Return to the Sea

John Egan

Return to the Sea

Acknowledgements

'Well Done, Mate' was first published in *Free Expression,* October 2015
'In Writing Class' in *Positive Words*, May 2016
'Taps' in *Positive Words*, August 2016
'Landing in Wollongong' in *The Mozzie*, January 2017
'Like a Patient' in *Valley Micropress*, New Zealand, April 2017
'Away' in *The Mozzie*, September 2017
'My, My, Hey, Hey' in *Valley Micropress*, September 2017
'Post Traumatic' in Poetry Matters 31, November 2017
'Welcome' in *The Mozzie*, December 2017
'Limits' in *Poetry Matters* 31, March 2018
'Ordinary' in *Positive Words*, July 2018
'Anaesthetic' in *The Mozzie*, August 2018
'Adverbs of Time' in *The Senior*, October 2018
'To the Right' in *The Mozzie*, October 2018
'Return to the Sea' in *Poetry Matters* 34, November 2018
'Cities of the Plain' in *Around the Table*, Poetry Alive anthology,
Ginninderra Press 2018
'Galaxies and Highways' in *Positive Words*, December 2018
'Angels of Dawn' in *Positive Words*, May 2019
'Toy Trains and Schoolgirls' in *Positive Words*, July 2019
'Archaeology of Weeds' in *Positive Words*, August 2019

For my wife, Marilyn

Return to the Sea
ISBN 978 1 76109 012 7
Copyright © text John Egan 2020
Cover image: *The Whirlpool*, Brenda Eldridge

First published 2020 by
GINNINDERRA PRESS
PO Box 3461 Port Adelaide 5015 Australia
www.ginninderrapress.com.au

Contents

Return to the Sea	9
Waves and Thunder	11
Flow	12
Yachts	13
Wolf-fish	14
A Sunday School Excursion	15
The Last Dreadnaught	19
Windows and Dragons	21
Symbolism of Doors	22
Airports	23
Doors	24
Away	25
Minutes and Hours	26
The Duke	27
Experience	29
The Shop	30
Remember	31
Cities of the Plain	33
Ghost Roads	34
Wasteland and Wind	35
Sensation	37
Quick March!	38
Welcome	39
Admit It	40
Anaesthetic	42
Recovery	43
Noises Off	44
Momentary	45
Creatures of the Night	46
Apart	47

Ordinary	48
Writing	50
Writing Group	51
Words and Music	53
Seashell	54
Tantrum	55
Like a Patient…	56
Not my Friend	57
An Archaeology of Weeds	58
Finishing Touches	59
Ties	60
Gold	61
Lorikeets on the Balcony	62
Screech and Bluster	63
Characters	64
My My, Hey Hey	65
Knuckles	66
The Glass	67
Toy Trains and Schoolgirls	69
Angels of Dawn	70
Chimes of Morning	71
Relatives	72
Full Moon	74
Galaxies and Highways	75
Starlight	76
Ultima Thule	77
And That's It	78
Post-traumatic	79
Landing in Wollongong	80
The Roxy	82
When	83
A Dreaming Dragon	85

Adverbs of Time	86
Lamplight	87
Walk Away	89
The Rose	90
Three Years	91
Redfern Genesis	92
Limits	93
Morning Brings…	95
The Eye of Storms	96
A Passenger's Complaint	97
Close the Door	98
Taps	99
Ice Cream	100
A Loose End	101
An Easy Mistake	103
Well Done, Mate	104
Goodnight, Malaysian Three Seven Zero	105

'For all at last returns to the sea – to Oceans, the ocean river, like the ever-flowing stream of time, the beginning and the end'

– Rachel Carson

Return to the Sea

The beach staggers
under a battering of waves,
broadens or shrinks away
from the sea's moods.

Whitecaps fly under the push
of the far wind
and a fraught horizon
meanders across your vision.

An onrush of breakers.
Waves pile into long barriers,
surge up to the air
like bloodrush, then

collapse under their own weight.
Spindrift's gossamer
flicked across the wind's face.
The mad weight

of foam on rock,
on sand and earth,
tumbles in a low orbit
and roils into cascades

on soft beaches, submissive
to its wild hammering.
Walk on a beach
and the sand keeps moving.

Keep walking
and you're absorbed by the sea,
its rising waters,
the impermanence of land.

Waves and Thunder

I came to the sea older than I was before
in a silence silent as the thunder,
asking questions no one cared to answer,
whose asking brought silent guffaws.

An unease of voices, the silent awe
when angels no longer sing forever.
You'll come to the sea older than you were before
in a silence silent as the thunder.

Listen to music, the words of songs and more,
listen to the sea and you'll find the answers
in the collapse of waves into spray and laughter.

Listen to the tides, their silent hiss and claw.
I came to the sea older than I was before,
and stood in a silence silent as the thunder.

Flow

Stand at the end of the wharf,
watch the river flow to the sea,
feel what its like just to be.

The force of the water dwarfs
the individual, you and me.
Stand at the end of the wharf

and allow yourself to morph
into the flow of the Chi,
feel yourself suddenly free
there at the end of the wharf.

Yachts

Billowing white sails
against the harbour's flatter blue.
Billowing white sails,
thin like harbour veils.
The wind whipped and threw
white waves and the black yachts flew
under billowing white sails.

Wolf-fish

A blue sheet strung between headlands
and stretched towards the horizon,
the sea taut and flat as canvass,
disturbed only by a trawler
moving at the pace of breathing
whose wake hardly disturbs the day.

Impossible to imagine what's below
like a woman's face smiling, her eyes
blue as laughter, teeth white as waves.
Off Japan, a wolf-fish two metres long,
whose mouth could swallow a small child,
caught like a leer beneath the smile.

A Sunday School Excursion

Scapa Flow, June 1919

Cleston Sound is flat as always,
this Sunday, quiet and clear, our navy
sailed this morning, exercises off the coast,
so the Flow welcomes only our steel tug,
Flying Petrel, gliding smoothly, her engines
chugging like a train down the strait.
Our Sunday school teacher, old Barton, says
we're lucky to be here on the water,
now the war's over and we can sail safely,
me on the upper deck, just below the bridge,
with mates like Tommy, Robby and Pete.
It's just great to be here and not at school.

When we round Midland Head, the whole Flow
opens up and north of Cava and there,
between Hoy and Cava as far as Risa,
neatly anchored, what we've come to see,
the whole German High Seas fleet, battleships,
and battlecruisers. They're ours now, huge, grey ships
that could have blown out towns to rubble
but our navy, much bigger than theirs
kept them locked up in harbour for the war,
except at Jutland, but we got them there
and they never came out again, too scared
says Old Bartie that we'd blow them to bits.

They're ours now. They've surrendered and we can do
anything we like with them, but not yet.
There's still Germans on board. I don't know why.
I can see *Derfflinger* and *Hindenburg*
and there's *Von Der Tann*, so sleek in the water.
The Hun called them *Panzerkreuzer*, leopard ships.
They say *Von Der Tann* can do twenty-eight knots.
No wonder our ships found them so hard to hit.
They sank *Queen Mary* and *Invincible*
and one other* I can't remember at Jutland
but we sank *Lutzow*, she went down,
and we got *Blücher* at Dogger Bank.
I can see them. They're spread in a long grey line,
right across our bows. Almost from shore to shore.
But they're so rusty, red streaks, huge splotches.
Some are more red than grey, like measles.
Not clean and well-kept like our ships.
I saw *Royal Oak* last week and she fairly sparkles.

Wow! To port! The Hun battleships, *Kaiserin*,
and *König Albert* and *Friedrich Der Grosse*,
their flagship, and further on *Bayern* and *Baden*.
They're rusty too and their decks strewn with junk.
We're turning north, must be after midday.

There's sailors all over *Friedrich Der Grosse*.
They're throwing kits and bags into those small boats
and some are getting in. They're rowing away. Why?
There's *Kronprinz Wilhelm* and she's tilting. Why?
Her bows are lifting. There's something wrong!
She's going down! By the stern! Oh jeez! What was that?
Like a crack! She's firing at us! They've got guns. No!
No! Her anchor chain's just torn in half.
Now she's rolling over. A whale. Huge and grey!
I can see her undersides. They're red.
Glaring down on us. It's paint, not rust.
And she's turning over. A great steel wall!
Against us. And she's just gone! Slid under
like a fish. Oh! Jonah's whale. Just for us.
Bayern's going down too. By the stern too!

Not a word, not a sound on our deck.
All I can think is…the Germans,
the Germans. They're sinking all,
all their own ships. They've sunk them. They're gone.
Rob and Tommy and Pete, they're just staring.
It's 3.30 and we're turning back.
I've been watching four hours, more,
and they've gone. Look around the Flow,
it's swept clean, red hulls above the water,
here and there, but nothing else. Battleships,
cruisers, destroyers…all gone. No. I can see
one ship, over there. They've saved *Baden*.
She's beached on Cava.
At least we've still got her.
The war's really over now.
All the German ships. They've gone.

* *Indefatigable*

The Last Dreadnought

Built as a compromise,
four Lion class battleships cancelled,
started because eight fifteen-inch guns
from obsolete battlecruisers had been stored
twenty years before, no need to build
new turrets, huge savings in time and cost.

Designed in the last year of peace,
laid down in the second year of war,
restarted twice, redesigned but far too deep
to pass through Suez, the largest
British battleship ever built,
two thousand men, her crew, hard lessons
learned from the war at sea.

A year too late for World War II,
she cost twelve million pounds
and was obsolete before completion.

Her one triumph, royal yacht
for George VI on tour to South Africa,
paid off to reserve after eight years, then
twice a film set, once a comedy
and once for a sea battle she'd missed by years.
Sold for scrap metal, only fourteen years old,
a fraction of what she'd cost.

The last modern British battleship
(the first dreadnought, fifty years before)
the big guns of every capital ship since
to hurl high explosives twenty miles,
armoured belts and steam turbines,
early twentieth-century sea power –
HMS *Vanguard*, for the Royal Navy,
the last dreadnought.

Windows and Dragons

Blue sky and clouds,
a tall tree, stone buildings,
framed in a dream
of silence and calm.

The world reduced to watercolour,
nothing here that couldn't date
from the nineteenth century,
a painting by Constable.

A dragon descending snarls
into the monstrous glass.
Claws extended, a flight
of snout and wings.

Reptile of wind, ghostly white,
a tail of bright blood,
the roar of turbofans,
a legend of arrival.

Symbolism of Doors

If open, come in.
If shut, perhaps
knock and come in,
but if locked,
of course, keep out.

To enter a room go through the door.
To leave go through the same door
but in a different direction.
Beginnings and endings.

If there's a door
there's a way in
but it's taking a chance
on the future – decisions,
success or failure,
happiness or misery.

I once knew a man
who, on seeing a notice
'Please knock and Enter',
on an office door,
did so
just to be cooperative.
His friend inside
threw a book at him.
Why not?

Airports

Airports are sad places,
arrive, depart, you're only passing here,
you're never there, perhaps even the fear
of leaving or the rare smiles on faces
at Arrivals. No traces
now of those who shed their tears
at airports.

There are queues but few social graces.
All hurry through or stare
at departure boards and care
only about flights to other places
at airports.

Doors

A video, Amsterdam Airport,
but shown years later,
passengers disembarking through entrances,
their journeys finished, perhaps coming home,
others embarking on new journeys,
perhaps leaving for years
through exits that take them away.

One young man rushing,
late for his flight,
running through Customs
anxious not to miss his flight home
after seven weeks as a tourist
in exotic countries. Boarding gates
about to shut, doors slamming.
He'd missed it…
but for one unidentified piece of luggage.

The flight delayed, the young man
relieved, boarding for KL.
Doors opened unexpectedly
for him and closed behind him.

The video shown only
to the relatives of those killed
on MH17
and only to those
who chose to see.

Away

Before you begin the journey
prepare your mind.
Stand on the platform, put your suitcase down.

Look to the west.
Follow the tracks to the setting sun,
to the mountains and beyond.

To the far side of the continent
where the tracks merge

into nowhere here.
Then you are free to go.

Minutes and Hours

Arrivals and departures,
the ticking of clocks,
footsteps.

The movement of trains
into and away from
terminal platforms,

the surging of crowds
like rivers
through the night.

The Duke

A 4-6-2 Pacific, Number 71000, *Duke of Gloucester*, was the last steam passenger locomotive built in Britain.

Prototype of a new class, express passenger
locomotives for British Rail,
always unique, the others never built.
In service, a total failure –
wouldn't steam, wouldn't pull, designed
for a Kylchap double exhaust, never fitted,
money saved, heavy on coal and water,
showered the trackside with soot and cinders,
clawed complete, unburned blocks of coal
through its tubes and hurled them out the stack.

Firemen preferred to take days off, lose pay,
than exhaust themselves on the impossible.
The last of steam, no point wasting money
to fix useless problems, the rush
to dieselise. Set aside early,
sold for scrap.

A change of luck – sent to Dai Woodham's famous
Barry scrapyard, sat among acres
of rusting hulks – new management policy –
cut up the freight wagons first,
leave the locomotives. Enough time
preservation societies to form,
raise money, buy the wrecks – rebuild,
restore, get them steaming again.

One hundred and sixty tons of locomotive
dismantled, just parts on the workshop floor.
No wonder she wouldn't steam,
a huge gap in the firebox joint,
a fault in construction, the whole system
never airtight, not enough draft
to force the fire.

Caprotti valve gear whirling, she made
the southbound climb from Carlisle,
fifteen miles of one-in-a-hundred
in seventeen minutes, a minute
faster than any previous engine.
'No problem at all!'

But the real test – the ascent to Shap.
After hours of hard steaming from Euston,
thirteen miles climb to Grayrigg,
then five miles sheer from the Lune Valley,
a barrier to every train on the Midland Route
since the line was built.
Wet rails, rain and high wind,
The Duke topped the summit
at over fifty. As the driver
eased the throttle, enough steam to lift
both safety valves, the boiler huge with steam.

Expert comment: '*The Duke* may not be
only the most powerful
steam passenger locomotive, but
the most powerful of any kind,
ever to run in Britain.'

Experience

A distant headlight
grows to an immense size,
the roar of steam and smoke,
a turmoil of driving wheels
and the pulse of pistons,
a face in goggles and cap
violating the night
and sleeping cars,
rolling into distance,
huge express on the midnight track
envelops all there is,
fading as love does.

The Shop

A cheap rack in a shop,
gloves, scarves, knitted beanies hanging
like the bodies of victims
tangled in the wreckage of a train.

The night express roars on, faces
and silhouettes in the windows,
garish in yellow light, haunted
by speed and thoughts of arrival.

Switched to a side track,
a slow freight in the passing loop.
Its engine simmers, scarved in steam,
firebox throwing red into the solid night.

The express roars on, the locomotive,
its huge impact erupts,
carriages splinter, brake vans
and boxcars crumple into chaos.

Before the collision, rows of faces
in windows haunted by the night.
Cheap scarves tangled on a rack,
hanging in rows, locked together.

Remember

Start your journey
towards a known destination,
a place you remember,
or at least
you think you do.

Streets of neat terrace houses,
a single-storey townscape,
doorways in lockstep
like sentinels in rows,
neighbours and equals.

This journey
becomes an exploration
into the unknown –
tall buildings that impose
a different status.

You're walking in the shadow
of crowds and strangers
glaring down from windows and terraces.
Sunk below their stares
you're diminished and uneasy.

A new panorama
sweeps away to the south,
a bowl of cityscape and distance.
A whole suburb
you never knew was there

leaves you breathless,
silent on the peak of a hill.
look away –
it takes time to absorb
a whole new world.

End your journey in a place
you've never seen before,
that's in your nerves now
that will be silken
in your memory.

Cities of the Plain

Tramp the fogbound highway into light.
Fix your eyes on the road, ignore
infections from surrounding night.

Memories seem merely wind on the sea,
wingbeats and angels in your head
and distant smoke, shadows of trees,

creatures of mire and monsters in the fens,
hauntings of light like horizon stars,
pale moonlight confused by the sheen of then.

Electric mist shimmers along the far road.
Domes radiant with light that burns away
the past and cancels every debt you've owed.

Your future hangs on a low horizon
and morning's merely hovering to meld
footsteps with the road you're marching on.

Night dissolves into morning and the sun
details the one black ribbon that flows
to silver towers, steps taken, one by one.

Ghost Roads

Where shadows fall, ghosts are walking
to remind us of the darkness
below the blue skies and sunlight,
to show us that the sun will soon be gone,

the earth settled back to its normal state,
when ghosts return to roaming undisturbed
in laneways. and in shopping malls,
public parks and the bush where their bodies

still dissolve in rivers, among foothills
and under the fencelines of farms
whose paddocks are never empty at night.
Lines of spirits that march the high ghostroads,

move with the slow rotation of the earth
towards the nothing we can only imagine.
In daylight, they cluster among long shadows
as if we can't see how the sun diminishes

like a candle that burns away
into thin photons between cold planets,
and the blackness they ever slide towards,
across the face of daylight spinning into time.

Wasteland and Wind

A cold wind, directly from the south.
Small houses in Redfern cling in rows,
streets of terraces neatly ordered,
one next to the other, for comfort and warmth.

Stop for a cappuccino and a rest,
a coffee shop sheltered in Bourke Street
where the plaza's deserted, bleak, windswept,
new buildings metallic, silver and glass.

At Danks Street, turn to the south, face the wind,
cap firmly on, scarf wound around your neck,
jacket zipped tight. You walk the long hill
that descends towards the far bay, the avenue

named for the Gadigal people, whose ghosts
toss restlessly in the wind around
apartment blocks, where factories once
marred the landscape and the air was foul.

Follow the avenue to its end, know
this area only by the names of streets.
Joynton Park, landscaped, peaceful. Here
you sat daily for weeks, a vacant

industrial warehouse, surrounded by
an empty complex, buildings and laneways,
the old Leyland Motor factory, already
closed, a vast space, filled with air and light.

You worked at a row of desks among many
who marked standardised test papers,
primary and high school, but here, now,
an alien townscape, disorienting

with panoramas of confused streets, where
Beaconsfield gives way to Rosebery, then
further south, Mascot, down to the glass waters
of the bay, where the wind sweeps from the south.

When you turn, walk warily towards
a shelter, for the comfort of any bus
back to familiar suburbs, you realise
you've walked miles and you've crossed decades.

Sensation

After Arthur Rimbaud

One evening in blue summer, I'll take the track
through fields of yellow wheat, over hills of lush grass.
I'll dream as the cool creek bathes my feet,
as the breeze streams through my hair, caresses my face.

I'll be silent, think of nothing, but feel
at one with the mystery of creation.
I'll wander very far, a vagabond
with the whole world as my girl, my lover.

Quick March!

Two lines of boys
in formal coats, bow-ties and top hats,
marching in ragged step
or trying to,
wooden replica rifles
over their left shoulders.
1914, a photo
of the Eton Officer Training Corps.
Sixteen-year-olds
playing at soldiers.

By 1918 how many
were still alive?

Welcome

As the defeated army
disembarked in Dover,
a volunteer
handing out drinks
for the broken men,
looked at a wounded soldier,
said, 'Well done, son.'

The boy stared back,
mumbled, 'Well done!
All we did was survive.'
The old man put his hand
on his sullen shoulder,
said,
'Lad, that was enough.'

Admit It

You set out
confidently enough.
Walk up the hill
you didn't even notice
when you were younger.

Think about longer strides,
deeper breaths, fill your lungs,
relax when you reach the top
and walk downhill,
easier now, past the shop,
around the corner,
but it's no good –
your breath's rasping
and there's a pain in your chest.

Stop, more deep breaths,
wait, force the air
into your lungs,
out of your stomach.
Watch the traffic.

You hate to admit this
but you just can't do it
you're only sixty-nine,
it's a mere ten-minute walk.
There's something wrong.

Make the decision,
push up the next slight hill
into the doctor's surgery.
There's a full waiting roam.
Tell the receptionist,
'Chest pains.'
She rushes you in.

Anaesthetic

It's a light switch.
One second, you're chatting amiably
with the theatre staff,
interested in what's happening,
wondering when they're going to start,

the next, light's back on
but you're in a different place entirely –
Recovery.
A nurse is smiling at you
and asking how you feel.

Now you're wondering
when you can go home.
What happened to you in between,
well, perhaps best
not to enquire too deeply.

Recovery

Listening to
three strata of noise
laid down in darkness.

The hum of air conditioners
outside my window,
the distant alarm
of someone's monitor
set to chime
at a specific reading,
constant, repetitive.

Closer, along the corridor,
a bell
ringing for a nurse
who's busy elsewhere.

It's hard to sleep
but if you're exhausted enough
you adjust.

It's good to know
even at three
in the morning,
things are happening
outside your dark room
and you're not alone.

Noises Off

If I listen to the rain
I hear two different sounds:
the clang of raindrops
on the metal chimney
carried down through the roof space

to the metal fireplace
next to my chair
and, at the other end of the house,
a cascade running as the rainwater
tank overflows.

Sometimes you're only aware
of great events
because of their consequences:
I cannot see the oceans rise
or hear time passing
or the universe expanding.

Momentary

In my driveway,
huge reflections of my headlights.
My neighbour's cat,
lightstorms in its eyes
visitor from an alien world.

Stop at the garage,
the cat vanished, darkness.
My headlights
showing merely brick and metal,
what exists not what I imagine.

Creatures of the Night

The night is alive with creatures,
weird creatures of the night
that hover near your face and fly
like birds but they are not birds.

They run like sand through an hourglass
and cry like children but are not children.
They never show themselves to you
but are there in the night, nonetheless.

Apart

I'm happy
when my wife's
at our house
in the country

and I'm at our apartment
in the city.
I miss her but I'm glad
the house has company

and the apartment
has a heart.
The house is her
outer shell

and the apartment
is the cave
I hide in
away from the world.

Ordinary

There used to be only
the one restaurant
which was excellent.

Now, the town's a tourist trap
and there are twenty,
all crowded,
most not worth visiting.

The best serves simple food
to differentiate itself
from more pretentious rivals.
I ordered what was really
steak and chips.

Look out its wide windows
at the serene waterfall,
the pool, water flowing
constantly into years
and memories.

My ordinary childhood.
After school, after homework,
Mum in the kitchen
cooking dinner, steak and chips,
for Dad, my brother, me.
Our dining room, our home,
my family.

The best restaurants,
no matter how modern,
always let me feel
I'm dining in the past.

Writing

It's digging your guts with claws,
probing into intestines
and running hot wires
through your nerves, testing your heart

for remnants there, drilling through layers
of embedded hurt and pain
into caverns and caves in the foundations
of sensations, under the pillars of now.

Writing Group

Tangible sadness.

Listen to your friends
read their excellent poems.
Comment, discuss, applaud,
criticise a little,
though not too much
and then…
You're next.

Why am I doing this?

Why sadness?
Fear of criticism?
But that's always welcome
to improve the second rate.

Is it more
the small poem that's so far
lived a sheltered life
in privacy and safety,
snug in the soft, quiet folder,
in a sort of warm, coddled adolescence,
will soon be exposed,
an untried actor,
a nervous singer,
and must perform as an adult
in the spotlight,
alone and unaided?

A sort of stage fright?
Or is it more
that all of the above
also apply to you?

Words and Music

In a few songs
the lyrics may not be
great poetry, may
even seem trite on the page,
but blend beautifully
with the music, the result
as close to perfection
as it's possible to get:
'Father and Son', 'Candle in the Wind',
'Waterloo Sunset'…

Seashell

From one side a wombat crouching,
but with green and yellow stripes.
From the other, a cartoon eye
dazzled in swirls, amazed by something
so weird, it just can't react
except by circles of confusion.

Summer, years ago, sitting, eating dinner,
a decade after we'd built the house,
my eyes starting from my head,
like a cartoon shell, a brown, fat
wombat, casual and calm,
walking past our window.

We knew they were there, had pondered
their droppings but hadn't seen one before.
Now we see them often, day and night,
not exactly like shells on the beach
but no longer with amazement.

Tantrum

A typhoon-trap
you lured me into
with smiles and pleasantries,
lured me to a headland
high above the sea,
with warm sun and friendly clouds.

Then your storm-surge struck,
attacked me with gales
and ice-bitter winds,
no shelter anywhere.
Your rain squalls spat at me,
hailstones hurled from the sea.

When I ran
desperate for shelter,
your cyclone
pelted my windows.

I'd reached the sanctuary
of home, dried myself
with warm towels,
still you stomped

and surged and shouted,
wild with word-winds
outside my door, me
bruised, battered, shaking.

Like a Patient…

Chattering at your back helplessly,
you just ignored me.
Your car sped away –

My nerves were numb as empty sky,
a freight train rolling
too fast on a single track
to change direction or stop.

The night trapped me,
shackled me, a prisoner
in a cell
built of your anger.

Shivering, shocked,
I walked to my own car,
anaesthetised
while you cut out my tongue.

Not my Friend

'I've never thought of you as my friend,
an acquaintance, perhaps, if you're lucky.
If you thought yourself a friend, well.
you've been living on another planet.'

If a friend is someone whose company
you enjoy, who writes you long, chatty emails
which you love to read and you always answer,
whose problems concern you, then why wouldn't I

consider you my friend? If a friend's just
somebody who keeps their distance or speaks
only when they're spoken to and always
about themselves, or at best, neutral subjects,

then just forget it, lady – life's too short.
I'm too passionate for bullshit like that.

An Archaeology of Weeds

It's a mess, offensive to the eye –
a green clump of god-knows-what.
A straggly rose bush, Wandering Jew
and something I don't know underneath.

Fetch the secateurs, the clippers.
First, cut the long strands of rose bush,
some dead, intertwined everywhere, rubber gloves,
a rake, yes, handle the stems gingerly.

Pull away the undergrowth and trim
the central tree, a pleasing shape now.
But the dead stalk on the other side,
cut it down, pull out the long grass around

and it's another small rose bush, alive.
What a find, but now for the weeds.
Reach under, clip the rubbish, pull it out,
handfuls of undergrowth – looks neater now.

There's a small trunk, another just behind –
two dwarf gardenias, remove
more weeds and clear a space around each shrub,
a little shaping and they're clean, neat bushes.

Then rake up, wheel loads of rubbish
down to the fireplace, stand back and admire.
It looks great, five shapely shrubs, almost new,
almost in line, space between them, space to grow.

Finishing Touches

Rearranged some of my veranda's pot plants,
moved one from a small broken pot
into a much larger one
where a beautiful old palm had died,

replanted some winter cactuses
into bigger pots and washed out
the old ones, scrubbed the tiles
where they'd stood for years,

swept, cleaned, tidied,
watered everything that I'd moved,
stood back and admired the effect.

That night it rained
and nature finished the job
I'd begun.

Ties

I wore a tie to work every day
for twenty-two years.

In summer, I wore a short-sleeved shirt
and shorts with long socks and a tie.
It was the fashion then.

In winter, I wore a jacket, a jumper,
and a long-sleeved business shirt
with, of course, the tie.

Later, I didn't have to wear one.
For eighteen years I went to work
without a tie. That was better.

Since I retired, I've worn one twice,
once for my mother's funeral, once for my father's.

My father wore a tie every day
for his entire working life,
even after he retired and didn't have to.

When he died, I took all his ties.
I keep them in a box in the garage.

They remind me of my past
and what I don't have to do now.

Gold

A crowded train,
coming down from the mountains,
almost on the plain,
rain and cloud
and to the south
a rainbow.

A little girl says,
'I've only ever seen
two rainbows – this one
and one in Thailand.
They say thay have gold
but I don't think so.'

I hope she sees
many more rainbows.

I've seen a lot myself
but never found any gold
and no matter how spectacular
they soon fade
to ordinary sky.

Lorikeets on the Balcony

Rainbow lorikeets chatter
as they're eating their food,
they just talk to each other.

Rainbow lorikeets chatter
like friends and partners who natter.
They're always in a good mood

so they just chatter
as they're eating their food.

Screech and Bluster

White cockatoos bluster across the sky.
Their ungainly flight gives reassurance.
Their clumsy flutter never slows a fast advance
but there is no elegance when they fly.

They reach the highest branches though may try
your patience if you admire a graceful stance.
White cockatoos bluster across the sky.
Their ungainly flight gives reassurance

that you don't need perfection just to fly.
Achievement's all, style may be mere appearance.
The white birds effortlessly make the merest

lazy effort and flash beyond your startled eye.
Though white cockatoos bluster across the sky
their ungainly flight gives loud assurance.

Characters

Obscure freedoms
of the heart,
embedded feelings
slow to move
but steadfast
in their journeys
to the fringes
of reality and love.

My My, Hey Hey

Neil Young sings:
It's better to burn out
than fade away.

Turn seventy, sit at home,
watch cartoons on TV,
every day.

It's better to burn out
than it is to rust.

Better the explosion
than trickling into dust.

Knuckles

Be the knuckle man,
get your knuckles dirty,
scraped, bloody.
Get the job done.

Be the knuckle man.
Your knuckles protrude
like nasty crossroads
where you change direction.

Be the knuckle man,
take the new path
that leads away
or leads home.

Your hands
are telling you
be the knuckle man
who gets the job done.

The Glass

The beginning of winter,
bleak and cold,
the curtains closed
so at eight in the morning
you think it's still six
and snuggle down cocooned
and warm. You think,
'There's nothing
to look forward to today.'
You roll over,
The glass is half empty.

The play you knew nothing about
ends, the actors bow.
There are tears in your eyes.
You leave the theatre
thinking, 'There is hope.'
The glass is half full.

A friend says something sharp
and you're discomforted,
not hurt
as you know
he didn't mean to upset you
but you think about it for days.
The glass is half empty again.

You receive the email
you've been looking forward to.
It says,
'I don't understand what you mean.
Please explain exactly.
I don't have the power
to read your mind.'
You reply,
say exactly what you think
and probably give offence.
You decide not to write again.

A card arrives
from someone else,
saying how much
you were missed.
Fill the glass.

Half empty, half full,
it doesn't matter.
It's both.
To someone dying of thirst
a glass half full
is everything.

Toy Trains and Schoolgirls

Never went to the Model Railway Fair.
At seventeen, at a school dance,
I met a nice girl, asked her out.
we spent a lovely day in Manly.

Her parents were divorced. During the week
she went to school, lived with her mother
in Haberfield, every second weekend
with her father, somewhere else.

A Saturday, going to the Model Railway Fair.
I took the bus along Parramatta Road,
walked a long way to her place.
She told me she wasn't allowed to go –

her father said, 'Too young for a boyfriend.'
She didn't seem upset. I was.
I went home and never saw her again,
I never saw the Model Railway Fair,

just lost interest after that.
Fifty years later, I'd like to go
but don't know when, or even if, it's held now
or where, certainly not Haberfield.

Angels of Dawn

Goodnight to you midnight ladies
and welcome you angels of dawn.
The night has floated into sleep
and the evening's delights have fled.

The willing girls are dressing now
and walking in their working clothes.
Goodnight to you midnight ladies
and welcome you angels of dawn.

The morning trains are leaving
and traffic builds on the roads.
Offices and shops are opening

and it's time to face the day.
Goodnight to you midnight ladies
and welcome you angels of dawn.

Chimes of Morning

Wake to the chimes of morning,
sunrise and a pristine state of mind.
The tides flow in at the end of dreaming,
whispers and feathers that float in the wind.

Consider the world's new breathing,
the bells and the echos of human kind.
Wake to the chimes of morning,
sunrise and a pristine state of mind.

The day's new lightshafts are forming
in the beckoning of waves and the blind,
wayward shafts of light, the hours when you find

your old and steady timepiece spinning.
Wake to the chimes of morning,
sunrise and a pristine state of mind.

Relatives

Homo sapiens, modern man,
is lord of the Earth,
it seems

but go back a mere
fifty thousand years –
Homo sapiens, yes,

but also
Homo Neanderthalensis,
Basal Eurasians,

Yamnaya,
Homo Floriensis,
Denisovans,

perhaps others we know
nothing of, all human,
the same species, sharing

the planet,
not ancestors, cousins.
No race is pure, all mixtures

of tribes, nations, peoples.
Most living humans,
Europeans, Asians,

especially
with fair skin,
freckles, red hair,

perhaps 3%
of our genes,
Neanderthal.

Full Moon

The moon intimidates the sky.
The earth succumbs to her beauty
like a mild, submissive lover.

She spins on her silent orbit
held by the earth's kindness and awe,
reflects love from another source,

produces nothing of her own,
is a tart who uses her man

but needs his protection and strength,
flatters him, hates him, cannot leave.

Galaxies and Highways

Stars like cities burn in the night,
constellations like highways
through deserts and lowlands
in the hollow sky.

The Milky Way's a giant
Ferris wheel that turns in a fairground
frenzied with speed and light.
We spin in its farthest spiral arm.

Andromeda's glow pinpoints
the human gaze as if
one star among millions
in its universe of far spirals.

Galaxies cluster and separate,
gravity in cascades, caravans
on the same thin highways, further
light years, the cities and the stars.

Starlight

The burning arms of darkness
and the red queen of the night,
if only their frozen verdicts might
reward your charade of meekness.

Despite your innocence and mildness
the moon dissolves in light.
The burning arms of darkness
and the red queen of the night.

All angels are cruel in their greatness,
in their malice and their spite,
in spells and incantations, in a bright

and growing red shift, starlight and its weakness.
The burning arms of darkness
and the red queen of the night.

Ultima Thule

The farthest object in the Solar System,
the very edge of the Kuiper Belt,
extremes of light, frozen rocks that never melt,
compact and stark, ghostlike emblem

of darkness and emptiness, the problem
of immense distances, mind-known, never felt.
The farthest object in the Solar System,
the very edge of the Kuiper Belt.

Dust and matter congregate, driven
by speed and gravity, huge forces dealt
by the hand of creation, spacetime welts

rock and ice, light fades, the mind riven.
The farthest object in the Solar System,
the very edge of the Kuiper Belt.

And That's It

The college is closing,
tomorrow.
Come in the morning,
clear out your desks,
take whatever belongs to you,
leave anything that belongs
to the college.

Your jobs are finished,
as from now
you're unemployed.
Thank you for your time.

This is 3.30,
just after the last class,
just before Christmas.

No thank you
for the last four years
I'd spent working there,
for others much longer.

Ain't free enterprise
just fucking wonderful.

Post-traumatic

After the hammer blow,
you still think clearly.
You grasp what's happened,
amplify the starkest details.
You're breathing. You sound normal
as you hear yourself answer questions,

but there's no feeling, nothing. You're
shackled in your empty bloodstream.
Ice thickens in your nerves,
crushes you in the crevasse
you've been hurled into.
Minutes freeze, hours, days.

Then the moment comes
when every neuron screeches.

Landing in Wollongong

Driving down to Wollongong's
like the final minutes of a flight
between the mountains and the sea.
Circling down from Bulli Tops,
Mount Ousley Road's direct approach
and 'Fasten Seatbelts' flashes for
everyone on board.

A matchbox town is scattered on
the narrow, low and coastal plain.
Roofs and streets appear
as if the map ascends
to three dimensions glancing through
thousands of feet of altitude.
Permission to land and then touch down,
fair and square the main North/South
beside the university.

A landing roll and brake to eighty –
the speed cameras lurk around
the turn-off sign to Gwinneville
and taxiways that lead off left
to North Beach International,
or further south to Crown Street's own
domestic terminal, plazas,
water features, shops and all
connecting buses through the town.

Australia's longest, thinnest city
squeezes low, abrupt and rugged
heaves of earth and stone, the scarp
of Great Dividing Range
along the softer, wave-crest scarps
plunging in from the great Pacific.

The expressway transits Wollongong.
The Prince's Highway wanders on –
Nowra, Narooma, Ulladulla,
Moruya, Bega and to Eden.
And there the irony of names –
from Wollongong to Eden in a day!
In myth, the Bible, history,
the journey's made the other way.

The Roxy

Rich, the scent of popcorn
like a rock song in the air,
Lucinda Williams, a burr of accent,
or something sour,
the energy of aroma,
offensive
but alluring in its popcorn way.

Air-conditioned, cool as a soft lilt,
the slight hum of machinery
like a backing singer
to the main voice, dim lights,
stress relieved as eyes relax,
as if the spotlight fades
and you're just standing there.

When

I sit drinking my tea.
I think of you.

Outside, a hot wind
batters the branches,
makes the day impossible.
It will be a long,
vicious summer, again.

This morning
I checked if your email
had finally come.
It hadn't.

Not hearing from you
is a hole in my heart
where you should be.

Away from you,
my life's a bleached
monotony of drought,
arid westerlies, oppressive heat,
meaningless.

Yesterday was your birthday.
You're a quarter of a century
younger than me.
I have your present
and the card with the poem
I wrote for you.

I want you to have them.
I want to look into your eyes
and see you smile again
I want to make you
smile again at me.

A Dreaming Dragon

I emailed you all the autumn
and you didn't once reply.
I rang you in the winter
then nothing, quietly said goodbye.

The sky was a dreaming dragon
and the midnight stars were cold.
I tortured myself to understand
you didn't want me, far too old.

I chilled my heart to accept
I'd never stroke your cheek again,
numbed myself to live without you,
unfeeling, alone like other men.

It's August now and still it's cold
but recently your email came.
We chattered childlike on the phone
and now I dare myself to claim

you might be my sweetheart still.
I hold your hand and stroke your arm
and the sky's a dreaming dragon
while the evening stars are warm.

Adverbs of Time

When I've been away from you
for what seems an eternity
and I'm missing you
like breathing,

every dark-haired woman
looks like you,
at first, then passes
into the nothingness

that isn't and wasn't,
will never be
like you

and I can start breathing
until I really see you
here, again, now.

Lamplight

Look out the window
into the confusion
of leaves and branches
where the great sequoia
smothers the night.
Look beyond the monopoly of glass
into the hollow darkness
where only the streetlight's thin reflection
guards the hours
like a nervous conscript
alone in the street.

Half hidden in the foliage
one other light only, the door lamp
of the building across the garden,
that I need to slide sideways
and look around the curtain
just to see but is always there.
It shines in the ocean of night
like a beacon or a lover.

So I think of you tonight, dark angel,
and our coming anniversary.
I've known you six years now,
though I see you, alas,
never frequently enough.

In the confusion of hours,
you shine like a beacon
in the hollow night, in my life
like the lamp in the garden,
not blatant or obvious
but always there.

Walk Away

We left the restaurant
and walked through the small, dark street
towards the brightness of Glebe Point Road,
where your friend was waiting.

My arm was around your shoulders.
I was stroking your hair,
a fall of soft darkness,
as we hugged and kissed goodbye.

I watched you walk into the bright,
your hair a shower
of black, gleaming, a torrent
under the city lights.

The Rose

I can forget how beautiful you are
in the usual context always there,
but a different place, a different setting,
you're more gorgeous than flowerburst.

A cafe, an ordinary grey skirt
and a coat with a fur collar
that pushes your hair up into a black mane.
You glow like sapphire in the light.

A short, black dress, your bare legs crossed,
your thighs displayed as you listen, smiling
and banter with, oh, so lucky me.
You a naked centrefold, sweet Venus,

goddess of the lounge room, goddess of sunburst.
You, Scorpio mistress of distance and dark.
You, glamorous in the farthest reaches of light,
beautiful, mysterious, as the dark rose.

Three Years

It's been three years but now you're back.
The world returns to its proper spin.
Now I comprehend the state I was in,
a cavern and a pit, my life cracked,

featureless and stale, deserted, flat.
today a better world begins.
It's been three years but now you're back.
The world returns to its proper spin.

I left you and you left me, lost track
of where you were though often pictured you, slim
in your costume, in your day clothes trim

as a photograph. I loved you, white and black,
for three long years and now you're back,
my world's returned to its proper spin.

Redfern Genesis

We met at the café. When you walked in
your smile lit the whole room,
a searchlight sweeping tables and chairs,
resting on me, a Hollywood star

in your spotlit eyes and you a rose
blooming in a garden overgrown
with weeds among dirt and stones.
When you walked towards me

it was morning in Eden, the sunburst
of creation and I was Adam reborn,
you Eve glowing in this drab,
ordinary café, a side street in Redfern.

Limits

Two worlds:
the window's shut,
the room's self-contained.
Even the sliding doors
are shut,
so there are limits
to what you can see.

Outside,
the world also appears
self-contained
within the wooden limits
of the window frame.

Move your head slightly
and the boundaries are different.
Move your chair
and the view changes.
Get up and walk
and a whole new world appears.

You can slide around the window,
peer out from different angles
but you can't see everything.

Open the window.
Climb out.
What's beyond that building?
What's beyond the horizon?

Just stretch a little further.
Be careful though!
Don't fall!
There are limits.

Morning Brings…

Music shimmers like sunlight
filtered through a screen.
The silver flash of mist and roses
flutters along the nerves.

Voices in the wind at sunrise
that whisper in the morning.
Thin guitars that linger in your thoughts
like the scent of flowers.

Midnight's lost on a highway
of yellow fog
and songs glow like petals
inked into your skin.

Music shimmers like sunlight
and the morning brings
its mad tattoo of memories
and roses red as blood.

The Eye of Storms

After 'Almost in an Album' – by Anna Akhmatova

'You will hear thunder and remember me'
as one who strode in the eye of storms.
The sky's rim will turn crimson as blood
and your heart will burn in lightning's flames.

That will be the day my narrative ends,
when at last I exact my leave of you
and scale the summits I have longed to reach
and see my shadow looming over you.

A Passenger's Complaint

It's a kind of death boarding a plane.
You're imprisoned there. You're never told
how long this night will be, how short the day.

Trapped inside a metal cylinder, they
cannot know the flightpath they're to go.
It's a kind of death inside a plane.

Your arrival seems a lifetime away.
Read a book, listen to music, watch a video.
How long this night will be, how short the day.'

What's out there? Dark clouds? Lights? Who can say.
What country's this? What cities there below?
It's a kind of death travelling by plane.

All you can do is sleep the hours away.
You're cramped, confined and bored to screaming, oh
how long this night has been, how short the day.

Reality is nowhere here. Your life's delayed,
a kind of halfway dreaming halts time's flow.
How long this night will be, how short the day.
It's a kind of death boarding a plane.

Close the Door

In the dark room Lucinda Williams sings
that you can never close the door on love.
The sleep of the mind, dreams that flutter like doves,
ghosts of highways, spirits inside of things,

the soul of words and the memories music brings.
Fill in the forms, tick all of the above
in the dark room where Lucinda Williams sings
you can never close the door on love.

Her songs arrow instincts and passions, fling
yearnings into notes, take your breath and shove
your promises and sweat and heat into the beloved

ceremonies of pledges and rings.
In the dark room Lucinda Williams sings
that you'll never close the door on love.

Taps

You rarely think about running water –
turn on the tap, it's just there, but our house
is many kilometres out of town, no pipes
for water, no dam, just fifteen thousand gallons
of concrete tank, gravity fed from roof
and gutter. An electric pump heaves it
into our pipes and taps. But when the power fails –

no pump, no water, dry taps and no bath
or shower, nothing to drink or wash, no flush
for the toilet, nothing. It happens rarely.

The twenty-first century and we store
our spare water in containers. The world's heating,
the landmass drying. How much water
will we need to store in twenty years?

Ice Cream

From my lounge chair
through the living room
and the glass sliding doors,
against the veranda

I see
explosions of ice cream flowers,
pink and strawberry bowls
of lolly shop azaleas.

A Loose End

I return to the school I left
when I was ten.
The old building, dated 1880,
was the whole school then,
now just the Infants –
three classrooms but bigger even
than I remember, cool, stately.
My mind remembered but my feelings
wouldn't respond, emotional
attachment lost in the sweep of years.

Only one memory. I stood
on the spot I'd hit out
at two bigger boys who'd bullied me
for weeks, threatened to 'bash me up'.
Dad had said, 'Just punch them
if they push you again'
and I did.

They complained to the teacher,
'He hit me!' as bullies always do
when their victims fight back.
The teacher looked at me, at them,
said, 'He's a good little boy.

He wouldn't do that.'
I often wondered if she'd seen
what really happened.
Now I know. Of course she did.
Her desk was really close
to where I stood.
That was sixty years ago.
Good to settle that in my mind.
I hope that teacher had a lovely life.

An Easy Mistake

An attractive, young, Chinese lady,
married, almost perfect English, my student.
'I'm Alison and I'm available!'

The first time she said it I let it slide.
The second time I had to correct her:
'Alison, in English, when you say "I'm available",

it means available for sex.'
Shock, consternation, laughter, 'Oh dear!
I meant I'm available to be friends.'

You can learn a new language perfectly
in class, but precise usage, then it's hard.

Well Done, Mate

London to Sydney direct,
20 hours 9 minutes in the air.
No passengers, no cargo, minimum crew,
a huge reserve of fuel
and a brand-new aircraft
stripped of useless weight.
Delivery flight.
The longest non-stop ever
by a commercial airliner.

The shortest flight ever
by a 747 –
Sydney to Albion Park,
flight time 12 minutes.
No passengers, no cargo, minimum crew,
hardly any fuel, an old aircraft
stripped of anything unnecessary.
Retirement flight.

VH-OJA, *City of Canberra*.
25 years of service.
The first Qantas 747-400.
The first flight and the last.
Two world records –
the same aircraft.

Goodnight, Malaysian Three Seven Zero

I've committed the perfect crime.
I've sought perfection and achieved it
and now I can die the perfect death.
The bodies of two hundred and thirty-eight
passengers and crew will never be found.
My body will never be found. My plane
will never be found. We've all just
disappeared from the world's radar screens,
vanished into the thinnest air, removed
by my own clever hands, locked onto
the controls, flying into darkness, into
mystery, into nothing, into nowhere.

I am alone. My first officer is dead.
I killed him, all my passengers, all my crew.
The cockpit is dark, except for the glow
from my screens and dials. the engines purring
under autopilot. I'm relaxed. It's quiet,
all communications gone. No one knows
where I am – I'm flying south-east
into the southern Indian Ocean.
I've passed the point where there's enough fuel
to reach the nearest land.

In a few hours, the engines will stop,
their fuel exhausted. I'll use
the auxiliary power, just enough
to guide the plane into a shallow glide
for a hundred, two hundred miles. I'll coax
her into a controlled ditching. She'll sink,
no wreckage to trace where we are.
We'll never be found. Goodnight,

Malaysian three seven zero. Goodnight.
It's easy to kill hundreds of people,
just turn off pressurisation, hurl the ship
into the tightest one-eighty to port, throw
them all out of their seats. In the darkness
they'll never find their oxygen masks.
Wait fifteen minutes. They're all dead
when all the oxygen runs out. Hypoxia,
the happiest of deaths. They felt nothing.

The stars glow like angels, the sea
solid black, at forty thousand feet clouds
below, but for miles ahead a clear sky,
the deepest Southern Ocean, where the swells
flow like fate and there is no land.
My instruments glow like old friends, their messages
of quiet comfort and the bowl of blackness
that drifts backwards past my windows.
Silence hums the hymn of planned, precise
annihilation.

www.ingramcontent.com/pod-product-compliance
Lightning Source LLC
Chambersburg PA
CBHW070936080526
44589CB00013B/1536